GARDEN SQUAD!

BUGS, PESTS, AND PLANTS

MOLLY MACK

PowerKiDS press™

New York

Published in 2016 by The Rosen Publishing Group, Inc.
29 East 21st Street, New York, NY 10010

First Edition

Editor: Sarah Machajewski
Book Design: Michael J. Flynn

Photo Credits: Cover (rabbit) LorraineHudgins/Shutterstock.com; cover (ladybug) PHOTO FUN/Shutterstock.com; back cover, pp. 3–4, 6, 11–16, 18–21, 23–24 (soil) Andrey_Kuzmin/Shutterstock.com; p. 5 Marya Kutuzova/Shutterstock.com; p. 7 Aygul Bulte/Shutterstock.com; p. 8 zcw/Shutterstock.com; p. 9 Meg Wallace Photography/Shutterstock.com; p. 10 Velychko/Shutterstock.com; p. 11 (seeds) Sebastian Radu/Shutterstock.com; p. 11 (seedlings) yuris/Shutterstock.com; p. 11 (adult plants) Hemerocallis/Shutterstock.com; p. 11 (flowers) CHAINFOTO24/Shutterstock.com; p. 11 (fruit) Denis and Yulia Pogostins/Shutterstock.com; p. 12 Alex_187/Shutterstock.com; p. 13 Chayatorn Laorattanavech/Shutterstock.com; p. 15 (ladybug) Jeff Baumgart/Shutterstock.com; p. 15 (praying mantis) S-F/Shutterstock.com; p. 17 Olivier Le Queinec/Shutterstock.com; p. 18 Kosobu/Shutterstock.com; p. 19 Gary Meszaros/Science Source/Getty Images; p. 21 (blueberry bush) BW Folsom/Shutterstock.com; p. 21 (fence) Agnieszka Jankowska/Shutterstock.com; p. 22 yuqun/Shutterstock.com.

Library of Congress Cataloging-in-Publication Data

Mack, Molly, author.
 Bugs, pests, and plants / Molly Mack.
    pages cm. — (Garden squad!)
 Includes bibliographical references and index.
 ISBN 978-1-4994-0941-3 (pbk.)
 ISBN 978-1-4994-0963-5 (6 pack)
 ISBN 978-1-4994-1006-8 (library binding)
 1. Gardening—Juvenile literature. I. Title. II. Series: Garden squad!
 SB457.M28 2015
 635—dc23
                              2015001794

Manufactured in the United States of America

CPSIA Compliance Information: Batch #WS15PK: For Further Information contact Rosen Publishing, New York, New York at 1-800-237-9932

CONTENTS

THE BUSY GARDEN

Gardening is a great way to have fun outside. It can also teach you a lot about the natural world. Gardening teaches us what plants need to live and grow and where our food comes from. There's more to gardening than just caring for plants. Gardens **attract** many animal visitors. Some are helpful. Others are bad news. They're called pests.

The bugs, pests, and plants found in a garden are interconnected. That means they need each other in some way. Let's dig in to this special garden **relationship**. Learning the basics can help you understand the busy world inside your garden.

What draws these critters into this garden?
Read on to find out!

CHOOSING PLANTS

A garden wouldn't be a garden without plants! There are thousands of plant species, or kinds, in the world. The ones you may put in your garden are those that can grow well in your area. This mostly **depends** on what the **climate** and soil are like where you live.

What kind of garden do you want to grow? Some gardeners grow green plants and bushes. Others may grow only flowers. Some gardeners plant vegetables, fruits, and **herbs**. There are many plants to choose from!

GARDEN GUIDE

Gardeners choose their type of garden based on what their interests are. People who want to grow and eat their own food grow fruits and veggies. People who love flowers may plant roses, tulips, or daisies.

The person who planted this garden is growing lots of tasty food.

THE LIFE CYCLE OF A PLANT

In order to raise healthy plants in your garden, you have to understand how they grow. Every plant has a life cycle. A life cycle is all the stages, or steps, a living creature goes through from the beginning of its life until it dies.

A plant's life cycle begins with a seed. To start a garden, you plant seeds in the ground and cover them with dirt. With enough water and sun, seeds sprout. They grow into tiny plants called seedlings. Seedlings are very **delicate**. When they pop up through the dirt, you must treat them with care.

All the plants here started out as seeds.

The seedlings in your garden will grow if you give them enough water and sun. Soon, they turn into adult plants—the next stage in their life cycle. Adult plants are your garden's shining stars. They have roots, stems, and leaves. Some plants have flowers and fruit.

A plant's fruit contains seeds. Gardeners use the seeds to grow new plants. Many gardeners take the seeds from the plants in their garden and plant them later. Some plants drop their seeds, and the new plants grow all by themselves. The plant life cycle gives your garden new life.

A fruit is the part of a plant that makes and contains seeds. Although we call peppers vegetables, they're fruit because they have seeds inside.

LIFE CYCLE OF A PEPPER PLANT

SEEDS

FRUITS

SEEDLINGS

FLOWERS

ADULT PLANTS

GARDEN FRIENDS

Good gardeners know that sunlight and water are **essential** for growing healthy plants. Great gardeners know there's something else just as important, even though they're kind of yucky—bugs!

Bees are one of your garden's best friends. They help make new plants. How? Bees like to visit the flowers in your garden. Flowers have nectar, which is a sweet liquid bees drink. When a bee lands on a flower, the flower's **pollen** sticks to its body. The bee carries the pollen to other flowers as it flies around. This is called pollination. Fruit can't grow without it!

Pollination is what helps plants make new seeds, which later become new plants. The bee shown here is covered in pollen, which it will carry to other plants.

GARDEN GUIDE

Pollination also happens by accident. Anything that brushes against a flower—such as birds, butterflies, and people—can carry pollen. The wind can carry pollen to other flowers, too.

THE LOVELY LADYBUG

Another bug gardeners love is the ladybug. Ladybugs are red with black spots. They're great garden friends because ladybugs eat other bugs. This helps control the amount of bugs in your garden—especially bugs that eat your plants!

Aphids are bugs that eat plants and can quickly destroy a garden. Ladybugs help gardens by eating aphids. A single ladybug can eat up to 5,000 aphids in its lifetime! Ladybugs also lay their eggs close to where aphids live. When ladybug eggs hatch, the **larvae** feed on aphids. Having ladybugs in your garden keeps it safe from bugs that harm it.

This ladybug is about to eat the aphids that are feeding on this plant. If the ladybug wasn't there, there would be one less plant and one unhappy gardener.

APHIOS

GARDEN GUIDE

The praying mantis is another garden bug that eats pests. They're great garden pals, too!

ATTRACTING FRIENDS

Bees, ladybugs, and praying mantises are very helpful in your garden. They each have a special job, whether it's helping the garden grow or keeping other bugs from eating it. The plants alone may bring these helpful bugs to your garden, but you can also make your garden very inviting to bugs.

Planting lots of flowers can help draw bees to your garden. This gives them a lot of food. Don't worry about being stung—bees in search of nectar are usually too busy to notice you. Another good gardening practice is watering your plants often, which gives water to the bugs, too.

GARDEN GUIDE

Some gardeners use chemicals called pesticides to keep harmful bugs away. However, they can also keep helpful bugs away.

This "bug hotel" was made to attract ladybugs and butterflies.

GARDEN ENEMIES

A healthy, full garden is something many gardeners enjoy. Bugs and other kinds of critters enjoy it, too. Gardens are a source of food and can be home to many creatures. Some of these creatures can ruin all your hard work. They're pests!

Many bugs are pests because they love to eat plants, and your garden is full of them. Aphids are one of a garden's biggest enemies. They suck the liquid out of plants, which causes them to die. Caterpillars are big pests, too. These pests chew holes in a garden's leaves.

GARDEN GUIDE

Beware of snails! They're common garden pests. They can chew through leaves, fruit, and even bark on woody plants.

These Japanese beetles have chowed down on one gardener's hard work.

A BIG PAIN

Gardeners work hard to fight tiny pests. There are big pests to worry about, too. They include animals such as rabbits, moles, gophers, birds, deer, and more. These pests like to eat the leaves off plants and berries off bushes. However, some, such as birds, eat bugs, too.

Like tiny pests, these large animals travel around looking for food. When they see your garden, they see a yummy and easy meal. Though these pests can be a pain, it's natural for them to visit your garden because it is a great source of food. Gardeners who understand this can work to keep pests away without harming them.

GARDEN GUIDE

Want to keep rabbits and deer out of your garden? Some gardeners spread human hair around their plants. The smell of people chases many critters away.

There's no way to keep your garden totally pest-free, but you can try to keep most of them out. Some gardeners build fences around their plants or put nets over them to keep pests away.

A SPECIAL COMMUNITY

Gardens are a favorite spot for many bugs and animals. Some creatures visit gardens to eat the plants. Other creatures visit gardens to eat the creatures that eat plants. Plants need bugs for pollination and to control harmful pests. However, some bugs and animals can harm a garden.

A garden's bugs, pests, and plants form a special community and help each other live and grow. However, this community couldn't survive without a gardener taking care of it. The next time you get out in your garden, see if you can spot some of these critters. Which are helpful? Which are pests?

GLOSSARY

attract: To draw in.

climate: The weather conditions in an area over a long period of time.

delicate: Easily broken or damaged.

depend: To rely.

essential: Needed.

herb: A plant with leaves, seeds, or flowers that are used to flavor food.

larvae: Bugs in an early life stage that have a wormlike form.

pollen: A fine powder made by plants that's needed to make new plants.

relationship: The way in which two objects are connected.

INDEX

WEBSITES

Due to the changing nature of Internet links, PowerKids Press has developed an online list of websites related to the subject of this book. This site is updated regularly. Please use this link to access the list: www.powerkidslinks.com/grdn/bugs